States of Matter

A Question and Answer Book

by Fiona Bayrock

Consultant:
Philip W. Hammer, PhD
Vice President, The Franklin Center
The Franklin Institute Science Museum
Philadelphia, Pennsylvania

Capstone
press

Mankato, Minnesota

Fact Finders is published by Capstone Press,
151 Good Counsel Drive, P.O. Box 669, Mankato, Minnesota 56002.
www.capstonepress.com

Library of Congress Cataloging-in-Publication Data
Bayrock, Fiona.
    States of matter: a question and answer book / by Fiona Bayrock.
    p. cm.—(Fact finders. Questions and answers. Physical science)
    Summary: "Introduces the composition of matter, its changing states, and the effects of
changing between states"—Provided by publisher.
    Includes bibliographical references and index.
    ISBN-13: 978-0-7368-5448-1 (hardcover)
    ISBN-10: 0-7368-5448-7 (hardcover)
    ISBN-13: 978-1-4296-0227-3 (softcover pbk.)
    ISBN-10: 1-4296-0227-9 (softcover pbk.)
    1. Matter—Constitution—Juvenile literature. 2. Matter—Properties—Juvenile
literature. I. Title. II. Series.
QC173.16.B39 2006
530—dc22   2005020127

Editorial Credits
Chris Harbo, editor; Juliette Peters, designer; Ted Williams and Anne McMullen, illustrators;
    Jo Miller, photo researcher; Scott Thoms, photo editor

Photo Credits
Capstone Press/Gary Sundermeyer, 7, 8; Karon Dubke, 4, 9, 10, 11, 13, 14 (all), 17, 29 (all)
Corbis/David Muench, 16; Matthias Kulka, 12; Michael Pole, 19; Peter M. Fisher, 6;
    Richard Cummins, 1; Richard T. Nowitz, 27; zefa/H. Spichtinger, 18
Getty Images Inc./The Image Bank/Angelo Cavalli, 5; Newsmakers/Spencer Platt, 15;
    Taxi/Kathy Collins, cover
Peter Arnold Inc./Bilderberg/UIF Boettcher, 23
Photo Researchers Inc./Frank Zullo, 26
UNICORN Stock Photos/Ed Harp, 20
Visuals Unlimited/Gerald & Buff Corsi, 25

1 2 3 4 5 6 11 10 09 08 07 06

Table of Contents

Features

What is matter?

Matter is anything that takes up space and has **mass**. That's a lot of stuff! Everything you touch is matter.

All matter you can see is made of **atoms**. These particles are too small to see one at a time. You can think of them as building blocks. Billions and billions of them join together to make things you can see.

Whether man-made or living, all things are made up of tiny atoms.

4

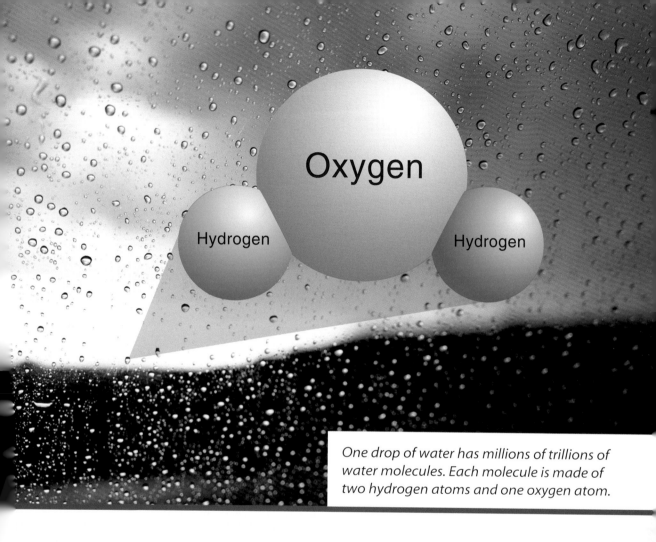

One drop of water has millions of trillions of water molecules. Each molecule is made of two hydrogen atoms and one oxygen atom.

One or more kinds of atoms join together to make **molecules**. For example, one molecule of water is made of two hydrogen atoms and one oxygen atom. It takes millions of trillions of water molecules to make one drop.

What are the most common kinds of matter on earth?

Almost all matter on earth is either a solid, a liquid, or a gas. These are called states of matter. Each state behaves in a different way. Solids keep their shapes. Liquids flow. Gases go anywhere they can.

Fact!

Your shadow is one thing you can see that is not made of matter! Why? Because a shadow has no mass.

Matter changes from one state to another when **energy** is added or taken away. Ice **melts** when heat energy is added to it. The water changes from a solid into a liquid. If water **boils**, it changes states from a liquid into a gas. When water **freezes**, it changes from a liquid into a solid.

Is air matter?

Yes it is! The air you breathe is a gas made of mostly nitrogen and oxygen atoms. Gas molecules are spread far apart and they move fast. Gas molecules zing past each other in all directions to fill the space inside a container.

Carbon dioxide gas fills a balloon when you blow it up.

Wave your hand back and forth to feel the invisible matter surrounding you.

The room you're sitting in is a large container. Gas molecules are bouncing off the walls and everything in the room—even you! Can you feel the millions of gas molecules that are bumping into your body right now? No? Then not enough are hitting you at once. Wave your hand back and forth. The wind you feel is air molecules bumping into you.

Why do we put liquid in a container?

Like gas molecules, liquid molecules also move around a lot. But liquid molecules move more slowly and are packed more closely together. Liquids flow because their molecules bump into each other and stick together. Then the molecules slide past each other again, only to stick to the next molecules they meet.

Fact!

The same amount of milk takes up the same amount of space in each glass. The shape of the milk changes to fit the container.

Juice takes the shape of the glass it's poured into.

A liquid flows to the bottom of a container and takes its shape. Without a container, a liquid flows anywhere it can. It spreads into a puddle.

Do the molecules in a solid move?

Yes! Molecules are always moving—even in solids. No kidding! They don't move very fast or very far, but they do move. In a solid, molecules are packed very closely together. It's difficult for them to move past each other. They stay joined to the same molecules for a long time. A solid has its own shape. It doesn't need a container.

Fact!

A crystal is a solid that forms when its molecules join together in a regular, repeating pattern. A diamond is a crystal made from carbon.

Both glasses have the same amount of water, but the water takes up more space as a solid.

Ice cubes take up more space than water because they are solids. Each cube has its own shape. A glass of ice cubes has air pockets between the cubes. The air and ice cubes together take up more space than the water alone.

What happens when ice melts?

Ice changes from a solid to a liquid as it melts. Heat energy makes the molecules move faster until they can no longer stick together. The molecules break free and slip past each other. The ice can't keep its solid shape. The liquid molecules begin to flow.

Heat from a burner melts ice from a solid state into a liquid state.

14

A worker spreads salt on a sidewalk to help ice and snow melt.

Each material has its own melting and freezing temperature. For example, salt water melts and freezes at lower temperatures than plain water. People sometimes sprinkle salt on icy sidewalks. The salt lowers the melting temperature of the ice. The ice melts faster than it would have without the salt.

How do puddles disappear on a hot sunny day?

Puddles eventually change from a liquid you can see into a gas you can't see. This change is called **evaporation**. Heat energy from the sun makes water molecules in the puddle move faster. Sometimes the molecules move so fast they zoom into the air. They leave the liquid to become water **vapor**. With enough heat energy, all of the water in the puddle will become a gas.

Damp rings around these puddles show how big they were before they started to evaporate.

Water vapor forms bubbles that rise to the surface as water boils.

Evaporation isn't the only way water changes from a liquid to a gas. When water boils, its molecules break free from each other. Bubbles of vapor form, rise to the surface, and let go into the air. Boiling takes more heat energy than evaporation does.

Why does water form on the outside of a glass of lemonade?

Water vapor molecules are always zipping through the air. As the air temperature cools, gas molecules lose energy. Eventually, the gas molecules slow down and stick to other molecules. They form tiny water drops. This change from a gas to a liquid is called **condensation**.

Fact!

Clouds, fog, dew, and mist are all formed by condensation.

On a hot day, water droplets condense on the outside of a cold drink.

Water vapor in the air loses heat energy when it bumps into the cold glass of lemonade. The molecules slow down and stick together on the glass. The drops start out very tiny. They grow larger as more molecules condense onto the glass. Eventually, the drops of condensation become too heavy and dribble down.

What does the weather have to do with states of matter?

Everything! If states of matter didn't change, we wouldn't have **precipitation** such as rain or snow. The weather is part of the water cycle. Water in puddles, lakes, and oceans changes from a liquid to a gas, thanks to the sun's energy. Water vapor rises and cools. It condenses into clouds of tiny water droplets. The droplets stick together and become large drops of rain that fall to earth.

Flowers need rain from earth's water cycle to grow.

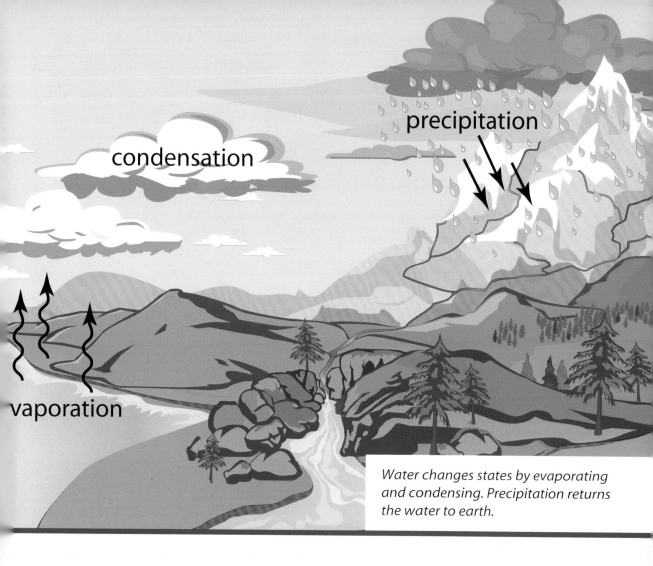

condensation

precipitation

vaporation

Water changes states by evaporating and condensing. Precipitation returns the water to earth.

Then the process starts all over again. The rainwater changes into vapor. The vapor changes into rain. The rain falls to earth, evaporates, condenses, and falls again. The water cycle never ends.

Can state-of-matter changes be undone?

Sometimes changes of state can be undone and sometimes they can't. When water goes from one state to another, what it's made of doesn't change. Its molecules are still made of two hydrogen atoms and one oxygen atom. These molecules are just arranged differently in solid, liquid, and gas forms. Water can change back and forth between states over and over again.

Fact!

Different kinds of matter change states at different temperatures. At 212 degrees Fahrenheit (100 degrees Celsius), water changes into a gas. But iron needs a lot more heat. It won't change into a gas until temperatures reach 4,982 degrees Fahrenheit (2,750 Celsius).

Wood changes states permanently when it burns. Its molecules break apart and can't rejoin to make wood again.

Sometimes materials form new substances when they change states. Wood burns instead of melting. Its molecules break apart. The atoms rejoin to make gas, water, and ash. These new substances cannot become wood again.

Why do icebergs float?

When most liquids freeze into a solid, they shrink. Their molecules pack more closely together and take up less space. They become more dense and sink. But not water! When water freezes, the molecules spread out and take up more space. Ice is less dense than water, so it floats in water. Icebergs are big chunks of ice, so they float in water too.

Fact!

Freshwater freezes at 32 degrees Fahrenheit (0 degrees Celsius), but salt water doesn't. The temperature must drop to 28.5 degrees Fahrenheit (minus 2 degrees Celsius) for salt water to freeze.

Icebergs float in the ocean because they are less dense than the water around them.

If water behaved like other liquids, cold ocean water would freeze and sink to the bottom. The sun wouldn't be able to reach the ice to melt it. The oceans around the North and South poles would freeze solid.

Is plasma a solid, a liquid, or a gas?

Actually, plasma is a fourth state of matter. Plasma is an electrically charged gas. It is the most common state of matter in the universe. But plasma is rarely found on earth. Plasma exists in things like the sun and lightning. Plasma is also what glows in a neon light when the electricity is turned on.

Fact!

All of the stars in our galaxy are made of plasma.

A neon light glows when electricity changes gas into plasma inside the light's glass tube.

Solids change to liquids and liquids change to gases when energy speeds up molecules. Adding lots and lots and LOTS more energy to a gas can make it change into plasma.

Fast Facts about States of Matter

- Everything you touch is made of matter—including you!

- All matter is made of particles too tiny to see called atoms.

- Most matter on earth is found in three states: solid, liquid, or gas. A fourth state of matter, plasma, is rare on earth.

- Gas molecules move fast and fill their container.

- Liquid molecules move a lot, and flow to the bottom of their container.

- Molecules in solids move very little. Each solid has its own shape.

- Weather on earth depends on water changing states.

- Some changes to the state of matter can be undone and some can't.

Hands On: Molecule Race

Molecules are always moving. See for yourself how molecules travel faster at higher temperatures than at colder temperatures.

What You Need

2 clear drinking glasses
hot water
cold water
food coloring

What You Do

1. *Fill one glass half-full of hot water. Fill the other glass half-full of cold water.*
2. *Let the glasses sit for a few minutes until the water is still.*
3. *Add one drop of food coloring to each glass.*
4. *Watch for several minutes to see what happens. Do not stir. Do not bump the table or glasses.*

Why did the food coloring spread out faster in the hot water than the cold water? Because the molecules in the hot water are moving faster. The molecules in the hot water bump into the food coloring more often than the molecules in the cold water, causing the color to spread out faster.

Glossary

atom (AT-uhm)—an element in its smallest form; atoms are too tiny to see.

boil (BOIL)—to heat water or another liquid until it bubbles; water changes from a liquid to a gas when it boils.

condensation (kon-den-SAY-shuhn)—the action of turning from a gas into a liquid

energy (EN-ur-jee)—the ability to move things or do work

evaporation (ee-VAP-uh-ray-shun)—the action of a liquid changing into a gas; heat causes water to evaporate.

freeze (FREEZ)—to change from a liquid to a solid; cooling temperatures cause water to freeze and become ice when the temperature falls to 32 degrees Fahrenheit (0 degrees Celsius).

mass (MASS)—the amount of material in an object

melt (MELT)—to change from a solid to a liquid; heat causes ice to melt and become liquid when the temperature rises to 32 degrees Fahrenheit (0 degrees Celsius).

molecule (MOL-uh-kyool)—two or more atoms of the same or different elements; a molecule is the smallest part of a compound that can be divided without a chemical change.

precipitation (pri-sip-i-TAY-shuhn)—water that falls from clouds to the earth's surface; precipitation can be rain, hail, sleet, or snow.

vapor (VAY-pur)—a gas made from something that is usually a liquid or solid at normal temperatures

Internet Sites

FactHound offers a safe, fun way to find Internet sites related to this book. All of the sites on FactHound have been researched by our staff.

Here's how:
1. Visit *www.facthound.com*
2. Type in this special code **0736854487** for age-appropriate sites. Or enter a search word related to this book for a more general search.
3. Click on the **Fetch It** button.

FactHound will fetch the best sites for you!

Read More

Lilly, Melinda. *Solid, Liquid, and Gas.* Read and Do Science. Vero Beach, Fla.: Rourke, 2004.

Royston, Angela. *Solids, Liquids, and Gasses.* My World of Science. Chicago: Heinemann, 2002.

Stille, Darlene R. *Matter and Material.* Science Around Us. Chanhassen, Minn.: Child's World, 2005.

Webster, Christine. *Matter.* First Facts. Our Physical World. Mankato, Minn.: Capstone Press, 2005.

Index